LETTERS TO EQUINOX

Dipika Krishnaswami

BookLeaf
Publishing

India | USA | UK

Letters to Equinox

© 2021 Dipika Krishnaswami

Presentation by *BookLeaf Publishing*

Web: www.bookleafpub.com

E-mail: info@bookleafpub.com

ISBN: 9789358738711

First edition 2021

. . .

On the night the autumn equinox is crossed,

Two stars we knew,

poised on the peak of mid-night

Will reach their zenith; stillness will be deep;

There will be stars over the place forever,

There will be stars forever, while we sleep.

-Sara Teasdale, Dark of the Moon

For my beautiful family.

Thank you for humoring my oddities

listening to my ramblings

reminding me of the things I should remember

and showing me how caring deeply is never wrong.

1. SLOW GROWTH

I wonder if she is color-blind, or was just
born without eyes.
What womb doomed one of us to never stand?
To never grasp? To never smile?
My stoppage of light spurs the emergence of her and I believe
she exists to remind me of how
I am not as transparent as I feel.

Midday marks her moodiness; she is stunted and she
threatens me with disappearance.
She attempts to shirk the curse of playing understudy to my
unbreakable bones.
She makes an enemy of my immunity
my refusal to fall ill.
She is a red-wine reduction
and she is too drunk to stand.

At the golden cue of late afternoon,
like clockwork blooms the death of my hamartia:
my fatal faith in the permanence of anything,
of her.
All my wasted worship for an aging God
gone like drought after cloudburst.

Because throughout the final hours of light,
she finally stands
She stretches her legs and grows
to boundless, beautiful lengths.
No longer a shadow, instead a shameless silhouette.

And by the time the moon comes out
and today turns to yesterday
again I am convinced that
we all walk amongst giants.

2.   THE SPEED OF TIME

Years pass like wet sand through slippery fingers.
Sometimes I can clings to pieces
or chunks will stay put
but grabbing greedy handfuls means
dropping the treasure;
quiet splatters on the muddy floor.

The questions you ask when
you know there will be no answers
are what I think soften the noise.
Like why time chose the pace it chose,
and why here, in this way, and not some other
and what sorts of judgements
will I pass in five years
and what will they say about who I still am

I used to spit over the side of foot bridges
just to watch my creation sail
from one side to the other.
Some days it would flow faster than other days
like some secret race I didn't know about

It turns out my resting pulse is
higher than average
I think that makes sense, judging from how
I like to live days faster than they want to play out.
Sometimes my heart agrees with my head.

I am on a quest for songs that force time to pause,
and breathe deeply in
if only to send smoke to the sky,
to take her unmatched hands
and hold them still for a moment
before signaling the start of strings
so confident on the down beat

I find myself searching for
reverse writings on steamy windows
like whispers from the universe
addressed to only me.
The trick, I've found, is to read them quickly
before hot breath smudges them away
over and over again.

3. THERE IS NO AFTER

If this is trust, then what is devotion?
Sacred sounds blasphemous rolling off razor teeth
I recall the clanging of bells and
the smell of smoked sacrifice
water dribbling down my forehead, carving canyons – brown,
dark brown
What will happen if I say I can't believe?

Rivers full of rocks flow slower
and there are no rainbows at night.
How does poison taste to you?
sweet sugar venom, afterburn of defeat
cheating death yields no winners
nothing but dust and dust again.
So how could you know fate?

Do I need scripture to be decent?
Hesitation is a habit, easy to kick
my choice, yet my back breaks from windup metal
my marionette limbs pulled apart at the socket
by dancing gloves in the sky
In the drama of it all,
I can never tell grin from grimace.
Who paid to watch me stumble?

Recited one thousand times
yet somehow never heard;

I am hope

I am horror

I am holy

4. SOME CIRCLES HAVE CORNERS

Some answers, I would drown for.
In salted sea or holy water,
it would not matter how blessed the bath was

Some mistakes, I would blind myself to fix.
I know there are one million lightbulbs waiting
for someone to find the right switch

Some people, I would follow through
sewage and storm.
They rarely deserve that kind of trust,
but I stay for the times they do

Some lies, I will always believe.
So maybe some circles have corners,
who am I to disagree

5. UNFORTUNATELY FINITE

She tried, I'll never say otherwise.

I'd yell that truth from heaven's rooftops if
it would make her believe that trying was enough.

I'd whisper it as a secret to every willing ear if
it would silence her regret.

I'd give her any star in the sky,
I'd let her pick her favorite.

I'd carry the whole world on my back if
it meant she could stand straight again.

She just wanted to turn sometimes into always.
I warned her that we will soon grow faint
like the blare of a distant parade.
She could not accept anything short of infinity

6. A CURE

I have a list of feelings which
I cannot put into words.
They drip down my back in streams of sweat,
and make my fragile hands tremble.
They fog my vision with dew and dust,
and so my thoughts turn numbingly wilted.
And perhaps sleeping will lead me to remedy,
but how rare a solution dreams are.

7. TAXIDERMY

What would it feel like to slowly unravel
to be meticulously resolved
knot, after knot,
as my thread frays slightly
desperately resisting a fast solution

I would take as much time as my
unraveling demanded until
I was a long, single string
a one-dimensional pinstripe retelling of my stories
stretched out exposing the stark nakedness of
each frizzy fiber and their garish display

It would not be the same as a dulling blaze
or blurred, vignetted corner

It would be a simplification of entanglement
a fated meeting with intertwinement's source

As I am gently laid on the ground,
amidst sights so painfully obvious,
so elegantly undone,
I hope my eyes have not already been closed for me.

8. SHOVEL

There's been some talk in the ether
They say none of it is clean enough
They say this dirt is permanent
It is not but filthy rot - the kind that leaves a stain

I scrub the same way I breathe
Purposely only when I notice it
This rhythm of scraping and scratching
Layer above layer of grime and grit

It is like digging a hole in the sand on the beach
right by the water's edge
A fresh flood with every attempt at excavation
The waves don't stop for even the most
passionate pursuit
But you'd drown before giving up

There is a gleaming screen at the edge of my sight
though it may be the same siren that
seduced so many others

It shows me an anonymous promise
It shows me a shore lined with sandcastles

It repeats a plea I recognize

'I know I may never be good,
but at least let me be happy'

9. PLEDGE OF A GRIEVANCE

I breathe with conviction and intent every day
I know how the wind churns, I know what he'll say

'It is i who blows without care of where,
through the thistle and bush and the curls of your hair'

I stand with the world on my shoulders but still
I'm shadowed by mountains and picturesque hills

They proclaim that they rose so strong from the ground
That when cities were lost in the quake, they were found

And I call to the world while I hover at the hem
And the bluest tides pulse and wave me to them

'Some salvation appears under feeble stars,
Like waves dance: wherever you go, there you are'

So I walked forever on paths I created
And pondered how different I could have been fated

I found myself right where I went, every time
Both my heartache's cremation and the scene of the crime

We're recycled at best, yet reborn to the earth
Hoping this time to find the truth of our worth

10. HERMIT

Abandoned does not equal ugly
that's what the stories of this place always told me
i listened to the secrets in the floorboards
and i collected rotting paint and red-brick mold
i kept crumbs in the cupboards and the bed sheets
and i gave my trust to the caving ceilings
i gifted my eyes to the warping blinds
and they returned to me a relentless rain that
i heard even with the curtains closed

if anything, my thoughts are the horrid ones
crusted into the back of my head like
dirt trapped under fingernails
i have given up wishing on fallen eyelashes
i will not say that Abandoned is built with
laughter and tender pastels
but Abandoned is not inhabitable
although i am alone here
i fear no ghosts or darkness
i dance for my mirrors, for an audience of one
for the creaky floors and closet doors-
i inhale both dust and incense

my breath can suffocate a candle's flame
but I know I can do more than kill
maybe if i paint the door to look pretty again
i will have more visitors

11. THERE ARE COLORS WE CAN'T SEE

On top of a building that I'm sure you've
walked by before
there is a concrete terrace with enough room for you and a
friend, probably
it is decorated with dried leaves, persistent weeds, and a bit of
splattered paint
and consistently smells like either trash bags
or cigarettes

You saw a chair up there once, remember?
It was wooden, and big, and
so obviously out of place
purposefully placed at an angle
facing an entirely unremarkable view

Since chairs are for sitting,
and you've never been one to question such truths,
you climbed to the roof to sit in the chair
as the noncommittal sky hesitated between
shades of orange

What you saw was people, unsurprisingly
and how they walked so fast, and looked so small
The dark descended like a slow curtain and
the four corners of your vision seemed to shift back
making the lamp-lit street and autumn moon feel like a lilting
dream

When the cold air began biting your bare arms
you decided it was time to go home.
The chair would be gone in the morning, of course
taking with it the tinted wash of life at a distance
and the hint of belief that maybe we're missing
half the picture

12. KEEPSAKE

A snow globe shatters when it is dropped
with an explosion of winter confetti
and an echoing shriek of some
murdered glassy memory

Call it reflex or call it grief
either way you're on your knees again
salvaging shards while muttering
a tune of inconvenient repentance

It's the tenth time, or maybe the hundredth
either way you're back for an encore
wondering how some cheap souvenir could cost you your
sanity, salvation, and
God damn Sunday morning

wondering who's admiring your shaken existence
watching white snow gently blanket the world
waiting to send it all back to the sky again

13. I SAW MY REFLECTION IN THE DARK

The room began to look like a flip-book
Flashing lights divided our limbs with
Fleeting moments of strobing black
But in between the inky still frames
We were happy

We were clarity while driving through downpour
We were the moment when the windshield is swiped clean,
Leaving behind a brief glimpse of direction
And the reassurance that we're somehow
still between the lines
We were a reminder of passing time
We were the ache of songs that sound like loss
We were the dreams we can't remember
in the morning

I saw ghosts in a hall of mirrors
They were all strangers who looked like me

14. MAYBE I'M BAD

In terms of the blades of grass
shouting sweet smells into the dusty wind
A desperate warning to their unknowing comrades
It is, in fact, the end, dear friends
I know it has been long awaited and romanticized as if it
would never really happen
A simple haircut, perhaps? Or the disposal of time encaptured
by those splitting ends
Floating aimlessly in a pool of trite phrases
They swirl and flow, lazy yet with intention
How simple it would be to reach out and
hold memories illustrated by words in
just the right sequence
Is there more power in the already-achieved
or the yet-to-be proven potential?
More questions exist on the backs of my hands than I'd ever
care to share
To recognize these knuckles in a criminal lineup seems
laughably unrealistic
These palms have held sin, and these fingers have carved both
love and contempt into tree trunks
and parted lips
I think I could be warned one thousand times about the
impossibility of untainted good
yet still question daily whether monsters
are created
or if I was simply less than remarkable
from the start

15. CANDID

Silhouettes of peace signs carelessly thrown
over slouch and shoulder linger for a moment
in the streetlight's hallowed cast
It seems as though the distant whisper of music
is intentionally synced to this dying thrill
Like a score for our Return to Stillness
A story tied up with both satin ribbon and
paper waste, splattered with tears,
mourning the way the credits roll over
something worth waiting for

       When will life smell this way again?
       I hesitate to ask for fear of an answer
       steeped in stained nostalgia

Now is good, I think I trust that
Now is developing in a darkroom
And I am being patient

The final shots are my favorite:

     the gentle flicker of lamp light through
        swaying leaves

     the shadowy wings of my open arms below

     the painless version of peace I've created

the moon watching from high above,
crescent and content

16. THE NEIGHBORHOOD WITCH

I know a woman who hung forks on her porch
Like a string of lights, or tinsel on evergreen.
When the breeze was especially strong, the forks would clink
and clash with each other, like wind chimes calling out to a
barren field
A genuine chorus of cutlery, no doubt
A sterling symphony: proudly silver and undeniably strange

When asked "why forks?"
she retorts "why not?"
With the same cadence and tempo as the asker.
This was her rendition of the Skeptic's Tone.
She was never met with a good enough answer for 'why not'
so we stopped asking 'why' so often.

When our questions stopped
all that was ordinary,
and all that decidedly wasn't,
and even all the rare extraordinary things,
blended and blurred together to reveal
a world so wonderfully odd.

I believe in absurdity like I believe in magic
Why else would a hat house a rabbit?

17. HAIKUS FOR HER PT. 1

When she brews her tea,
sweet spices softly steep as
she turns dirt to gold.

she loves like the sky:
skin of stars, thoughts of thunder;
my infinity

magic mirror girl:
her eyes reflect horrors that
I've tried to forget.

18. HAIKUS FOR HER PT. 2

washing blood off hands
and pretending not to see
are one and the same

what choice is there now
but to bury all the mess
our meddling hands made

you jumped off the edge
but gravity's who helped you fall
screaming won't stop time.

19. ALONE, ONCE MORE

Every ending you experience is
only truly The End
If you are under the impression that
this story was ever about you.

It's the silence of an empty house
and the stench of self neglect
that leave that burnt taste in your mouth,
I promise
It's not the things that could have been
or the words you couldn't say.
They smell of birthday cake, clean hair,
cheap beer, and dish soap;
not burning.

I hug myself at night sometimes
when my bed is especially cold.
I know I'll wake up warm in my arms.

I know that I'll wake up.

20. 7 AM IS ALWAYS THE SAME

bus stop pacing
bad breath tasting
balled up fist in one pocket,
middle finger in the other
muzzle on too tight
eyebrows scrunched like spare dollar bills
candy wrapper, tumbling and ripped
wind whipped hair stuck to lips
early sounds of yawning
coughing and rubbing eyes
watch checked 10 times a minute
eyes darting to the beat of drums
pounding in the morning fog

the bus is late today, the bus is always late
with nowhere else to be, why not wait

why not wait

21. A LIST OF RULES OR
UNREASONABLE REQUESTS

Always remember to knock.
Brush your teeth before breakfast.
Laugh at my good jokes.
Laugh harder at my bad jokes.
Play music at the volume the song deserves.
Say yes when I ask for dessert.
Leave the toilet seat down.
React the right way when I'm excited.
Call my phone only for emergencies.
Hold my hand till it's sweaty (then you can let go).
Offer to drive so I can just sit next to you.
Notice when I'm sad, and let me be that way.
Make fun of me in small doses.
Ask me if I've eaten today.
Let me shower you in compliments when you're full of doubt.
If you say you will stay, then stay.
Say sorry only if you mean it.
Remember the smallest things, and the biggest things too.
Realize that I'm flawed (arguably beyond repair),
but choose not to mind because of
all my good parts.
Admire the stars with me.
Tell me the secrets you hide from the rest.
Remind me that hope is as constant as pain.

Make the existing seem right.

Don't be afraid if I ask for too much.

22. DEFROSTING DAY

the snow performs a dance
like a gentle rebirth:
calmly reminding us that
there is beauty in falling down
just as much as there is
in standing up again.

the ground welcomes this frozen white
knowing that while it will hide for a time
it will also re-appear;
thawed and awake and
so much more vibrant than before.

23. LEAD PIPES

I'm never surprised when you lie anymore.
You've burned bridges before they were even fully built, so
each new fire is
nothing but a re-scorch

I'm not sure if you meant to impress or
if it was all just a bad joke you were told as a kid

You inhaled your world like threatened breath
and gnashed it into a blackened tar
stinking of dirt and disguise
and you retched that bloody bile into box and bow
and smiled the way gift-givers do

I listen to you speak the way I drink from
lead pipes.

I'm still thirsty, but I know a
second glass could kill.
I'm still trying, but I know a
second chance could kill.

24. CONCLUSIONS OF A CYNIC

There's much to say about the chase
and the dodging of falling rocks
the clumsy handoff during the race
and the bricks mistaken for stumbling blocks

There's fear and delusion fighting their fight,
commonplace in this kingdom of rats
the sun must sleep, but we wake out of spite
to go hill hunting in the Valley of Flats

Like the first thought when things fall silent
or the sound between droplets of rain
I can't help but wonder where all the wonder went
I haven't found one willing to explain

The vigilant avoidance of quicksand
and half-skip up the grassy hill
the opening and swallowing is rarely planned
yet the ever-emptying glass remains filled

You can ask your questions and spill your lies
in the strangest places lives what is true
but where do you keep the memories
that have all but died –
in the next-to-noiseless chamber of you?

25. ALMOST ORION

I wish to be dotted with freckles and spots

To be a pointillist exhibition, a gallery-goer's thrill
To be both muse and canvas
both portrait and landscape,
adorned by the same gifted brush who
constellated such starry nights

I wish to be traced with fingers and eyes
seeking patterns that may lead them to fate

Sketched skyfulls are known to refuse replication -
any scribble on my skin resembling the celestial
would be nothing but a glorious glitch of creation

I wish to be a replica of those drawings in the dark
I wish to be speckled with stars

26. SO THE RUMORS WERE TRUE

Someone once told me you were nature's
finest blossom
and I didn't believe them, how could I
for I have seen the moody blooms kindly
show winter the door,
seen them struggle up out of the dirt with a hope only
dormancy could create
I have heard the sounds of growing things,
all the creaks and groans the tree trunks make
as their naked limbs stretch and shiver
I have heard the words of the wind,
and his voice sounds nothing like yours

But how quickly you put sunshine to shame
made clear to me that you were artwork
told me it was ok to stare.

Though, I already knew not to touch.
I knew never to meddle with masterpiece.

27. A MEASUREMENT OF TRUST

It is early, and the sun is carefully
whittling her way through the cracks of the blinds
and the curtains give way to her weight
my eyes are foggy, like the misted morning
and my bones are tight from curling up
with the moon.
I stretch, blink hard twice, and notice the way the light
waltzes on my fingers when I reach
up to the ceiling.
The day is opening like the front cover of a novel and my
brain is still dim
the lights are turned down to a whisper
and no matter the brightness of the sun today
they will remain soft - so frustratingly quiet.
I sit up and stretch once more to shake off
any leftover dreamstuff
here, between four walls, two windows,
and barely enough space,
the world is softly raining
and candle-flame will never turn to lightening but
I still hear thunder, again and again.

I pour my coffee too eager
and fill it too far
nearly killing the brim.
I waste some and
feed it to a patient drain.

Just as I did yesterday
and so many days before
I hold a mug only three quarters full
and I let both my hands soak up a
temporary warmth

This one is a memorized measurement;
enough room for a splash of cream and a sunrise

28. I'D RATHER BE CREMATED

I think about pinning our photo
to the wall in my room
in front of my favorite south-facing window
so that the glossy print bleeds into the paint
and the colors of our clothes age like milk
and dust coats the memory in a filthy skin
and our smiles fade like well-loved summer denim.

I think about the version of us held hostage in time:
savoring an expired countdown and flash
by overdosing on unfiltered sunlight

I think each gold-poisoned drop will
bring us one page closer
to an epilogue that preserves our stories
in the small space between our names

29. DANGLING BY A CLOTHESPIN

This barely-ticking hour dries so slow
half-clipped, half-draped on laundry line
damp linen basking in steady heat-
every inch knows real thirst
each minute collects fresh blisters
tissues pass like crumpled tumbleweed
smearing evidence all over the lawn
proving years of hoarded ichor and tears

Like frostbite only worsens with time,
the daylight grows selfish come solstice
and I'm left squinting at a blurred horizon
making bets with withered leaves on
if I'll be around this time next year

I'd like to hear a delicate begging
a request smothered by sun-dried sheets
I could be some leaving lover, looking
back at an unmade bed

stay here, please
I gambled so much on you
don't go

30. THE ONLY CHANNEL ON TV

It's late, but we are just in time for Moonshow

I'm frantically gathering your favorite snacks

You're fumbling for the remote in

the light of TV static

By the time the picture pixelates before us

We are snug, our feet tangled up, our hands

gently brushing

both accidentally and on purpose

The couch is the perfect distance from

our sacred screen

And we are surrounded by rocks more priceless than

palladium

We tuck our belongings into hollowed ground

As if decorating holes could make a stone feel like home

Moonshow begins with the same familiar tune

and a glorious vision of blue and green

glowing like a beautiful stranger

so far out of reach, but here before our eyes

We watch with a longing sweetened by comfort

Moonshow is pressing a cup to our ears and

hearing a voice from the other end of the string.

Moonshow means we have not yet been forgotten.

Without distractions,

or clouds to watch go by,

we've almost run out of stars to wish upon.

It's true the nights here last forever,

but I think it's better this way.